THIS BOOK BELONGS TO

Love

Love

www.ingramcontent.com/pod-product-compliance
Lightning Source LLC
Chambersburg PA
CBHW081725220526
45468CB00008B/1972